Praise for Taming the Social Media Monster

"A great overview of the social media challenge many businesses are facing. A smart, well-researched, and easy-to-read guide for anyone fumbling around in the new world of social media marketing and community-building. If you haven't been able to 'get your head around' this new way of communicating and connecting with your potential customers, reading this guide will point you in the right direction."

> ~ Ken Kesslin, President, Kesslin Associates
> www.kesslin.com

"As the CEO of a leadership development firm I am always looking for great resources for my clients. As soon as I saw the critical errors and read these do-able, concrete ideas for managing social media I got very excited! Thanks for this fantastic resource. Just what we need right now! A simple, clear, immediately useful guide to the way we interact with consumers in a new era of two-way communication. Examples like the U.S. Army can help us reduce our fear, and realize it's not a monster after all!"

> ~ Karlin Sloan, CEO, speaker, and author of Smarter Faster, Betterand Unfear; Facing Change in an Era of Uncertainty. www.karlinsloan.com

"As a veteran of the social media industry – and it does move fast – I was still able to gain some valuable gems out of this book. Whether you are new to social media or an advanced marketer, this book is a must read. While most books on the topic are a heavy read, Taming the Social Media Monster, is quick, fun, AND entertaining. Pick up a copy today. You can't go wrong."

> ~ Shama Kabani, Author of the Best-Selling The Zen of Social Media Marketing. www.marketingzen.com

"A must-read for business executives! While there is vast information on the spread of social media, most is hype, encouraging businesses to simply "jump on the bandwagon". I work with many CEOs and find that many are skeptical of social media because of the hype. Pomerantz & Burmeister provide a no-nonsense approach to finding solutions that fit and support your business strategy. Read this and you'll be able to see clearly where you need to focus."

~ Lee Self – President, Renaissance Executive Forums
http://www.executiveforums.com/lself

"Taming the Social Media Monster is a clear and concise discussion on issues and - most importantly - solutions on how to successfully introduce and integrate social media into your workplace. A must have book for all businesses."

~ Dede Haas, Managing Director, The Unicorn Group

"Taming the Social Media Monster is a must read for anyone in business today. The book provides great insight not only into the power of social media, but the bottom line benefits it can bring to those businesses willing to invest in a strategy. In every chapter, the authors give you practical information, and easily implemented ideas and techniques. I plan to keep this book on hand, and use it as my guide to not only tame but master the Social Media Monster!"

~ Meridith Elliott Powell - Coach, Speaker, Business
Development Expert, Author of "42 Rules To Turn
Your Prospects Into Customers"

"Very cool book. Concise (at 50 pages) and to the point on a growing important subject: Social Media. This is something CEOs might actually read! Made me think about what I was and was not doing that I should and should not be doing regarding social media."

~ Steve Gladis, Ph.D., CEO and Author of 15 books on
leadership http://survivalleadership.blogspot.com

Taming The Social Media Monster

Solutions

To The 5 Biggest Mistakes

Companies Make

Suzi Pomerantz

Misti Burmeister

Published 2010 as an eBook by
Innovative Leadership International LLC and Inspirion LLC

Published 2011 by: Innovative Leadership International LLC

ISBN-13: 978-1460931615
ISBN-10: 1460931610

This publication is designed to provide accurate and authoritative information with regard to the subject matter covered. It is sold with the understanding that neither the author nor the publisher is engaged in rendering legal, accounting, or other professional service. If legal advice or other expert assistance is required, the services of a competent professional person should be sought.

> — From a Declaration of Principles jointly adopted
> by a Committee of the American Bar Association
> and a Committee of Publishers and Associations

Editorial services by Leslee Johnson
eBook formatting and cover design by Exceptional Business Solutions, Inc.
Book design and formatting by Sandra Larson Design

Available through SuziPomerantz.com

"How can you squander even one more day not

taking advantage of the greatest shifts of our generation?

How dare you settle for less when

the world has made it so easy for you to be remarkable?"

~ Seth Godin, Seth's Blog

DEDICATION

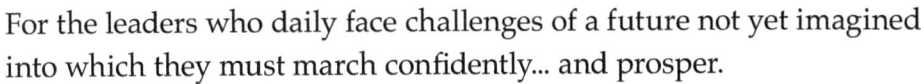

For the leaders who daily face challenges of a future not yet imagined into which they must march confidently... and prosper.

For the courageous leaders who seek new avenues for innovation and see possibility everywhere.

For the new breed of leaders who embrace a world moving at the speed of technology.

This book is dedicated to you, the leaders.

Table of Contents

INTRODUCTION:
Why We Must Confront
The Social Media Monster

INTRODUCTION:
Why We Must Confront The Social Media Monster

Like the magic dragon in a fairy tale, social media has grown exponentially large in a very short time. Facebook, Twitter and LinkedIn, popular platforms people use to connect with one another socially and professionally, are now household names. If you don't know a tweet[1] from an email, or a friend from a fan[2], it will benefit you and your organization to learn the basics. What we affectionately refer to as "the social media monster" is quickly taking over the relationships you have with your employees and customers, vendors and stakeholders, media and prospects.

The Nielsen Company, in April 2009, found that Americans spent 73 percent more time on social networking sites than in 2008. Unfortunately, the huge popularity and voracious hunger with which people follow social media has some business leaders scratching their heads, or running for cover.

Time management, security issues, reputation risk, and the complicated logistics of developing a strategy for utilizing social media are executives' main concerns.

---

[1] A "tweet: is a communication on Twitter, usually no more than one sentence; a post that is limited to 140 characters in length. Content for tweets might consist of "status updates," of how/ what a person is doing at any given moment, although the most powerful use of Twitter is the connections made by posting deep thoughts, offering help to others, and sharing quality content with others. Tweets can also include links in the form of shortened urls to sites or clogs of interest to the user and their "followers." (i.e. those who receive their tweets.)

[2] A "friend" is someone users acknowledge on Facebook as part of their virtual community, and can be either a real life friend or simply an online acquaintance dubbed "friend" in the world of Facebook. A "fan" is someone who identifies with a product, company or brand and created or joins a Facebook page dedicated to that product, company or brand.

"My employees spend an exorbitant amount of time on social media," complains a Fortune 500 executive. "How do I get them to stay focused on work while they're in the office?"

"We have real security issues to be concerned with," notes a high-level military leader. "Social media is an animal I'm not sure how to cage!"

A government contractor CEO observes, "We need to create some sort of system for dealing with social media. Can we prove that the potential benefits of a social media strategy outweigh the risks?"

As with all forms of communication, social media can be a powerful tool for both employee and customer engagement. It can also become the cause of much debate and consume the precious time of all those involved. The concerns of high level leaders are valid, and the enthusiasm of those employees already utilizing the various social media platforms may seem, to the less tech-savvy executives, to be disconnected from the core mission of the business.

Social media resembles a mystical monster more than a controllable tool. How does a company tame the monster and tap into the huge market social media reaches? This book is designed to answer this question and address the issues companies face when trying to leverage social media and harness its colossal power.

While some companies reject the notion of social media altogether, other companies dive in headfirst without fully recognizing the consequences. "Companies identify social media as a key communications strategy, but few are adequately addressing concerns regarding corporate security and reputational risk," said relevance management specialist Russell Herder in a 2009 study.

The research reported that "more than eight in 10 executives said they have concerns about social media and its implications for both corporate security and reputation management. Yet, surprisingly, only one in three said they have implemented social media guidelines and only 10 percent have undertaken related employee training."

While the risks are clear and present, the advantages social media offers are even stronger when approached from the right perspective. For example, there is a proven correlation between financial performance and social media engagement. According to a study of the usage of social media among Inc. 500 companies by the Center for Marketing Research at the University of Massachusetts Dartmouth, "the 2009 results confirm that the fastest growing private companies adopt social media marketing initiatives at much higher rates than other companies."

An effective social media strategy can help you:

- Promote your brand

- Get qualified feedback

- Improve search engine optimization

- Recruit new talent

- Engage with customers

- Obtain valuable market research for free by listening to what customers are saying in social media outlets.

So, can you leverage the power of Twitter, Facebook and other social media platforms in a way that aligns with and relates to your business strategy?

Can you utilize social media in a way that keeps employees focused and engaged on the mission and work of your organization?

Is it possible to increase productivity, employee engagement, ensure proper company branding and get the most out of social media?

Can you create clear policies and strategies for communication regarding the use of social media so that employees understand the implications of such resources?

Absolutely!

Throughout the following five chapters, we address those important questions and outline the most common challenges companies face with social media. Beyond simply defining the challenges, we also outline clear and efficient ways of dealing with these top five challenges.

Soren Gordhamer, author of Wisdom 2.0 writes, "Social media is helping to forge a new era in business transparency and engagement, creating both new challenges and opportunities. Companies now face a clear choice: wall themselves in and become increasingly controlled and hidden, or use social media and other means to reveal their human side, welcome transparency, and forge new relationships with their customers. The old game is undoubtedly over, and the question now is, 'What can businesses do to transition and succeed in this new era?'"

Effective use of social media platforms has the potential to update and revolutionize your company's systems of communication, marketing and management. In facing the social media monster, you have nothing to lose and much to gain in productivity, customer satisfaction, and a healthier, happier organization.

Within this book you will find the tools, steps and resources necessary to tame the monster and put social media to work for your bottom line.

Chapter One:
STRATEGY

The social media revolution has

irreversibly changed the way we live

our lives and conduct our business.

Chapter 1: STRATEGY

Should you embrace change and capitalize on new technology or ban it for fear of all the problems it could cause? Does social media really decrease productivity, cause reason for security concerns and ultimately waste time, energy and resources? It could, if you don't have a clear plan and ensure everyone is on board. With a solid strategy in place, social media can be leveraged to amplify and broadcast all the good things your organization is doing.

If you think you can ignore social media and wait for the fad to pass, think again. This monster is not going to magically disappear. You can't avoid it any longer. In fact, if you do bury your head in the sand, you're likely to be left behind, or swallowed up, as the various technologies evolve. Getting in the social media game now can save you and your organization a lot of pain and cost down the road.

Your role as leader is impacted by the age of social media. The dynamics of business communication are forever changed. Now is the time to evaluate how your company can take advantage of the exciting new venues and opportunities social media has to offer.

But rather than leap headfirst into the huge virtual arena, companies that are successful with social media have taken the time to develop a solid strategy, one which aligns with their mission and vision and includes both their human resources and their consumers.

CRITICAL ERROR #1: Lack Of A Unified Strategy

As with any new initiative, technology is best used with a clear plan and objective. Many companies (small and large) hear about a new form of technology and jump on the bandwagon without first creating a plan. Then, after a few months, they don't understand why they haven't gotten anywhere with the new technology, even though they never created a "there," or a plan for the use of the technology.

If your company were preparing to launch a new product or service, you would likely create a marketing and/or advertising plan. Over the course of several months, maybe even a year, you would begin working the plan, making adjustments along the way. It's doubtful any company would put money into building something and never let anyone know about it. However, this lack of strategy is just what many high-profile companies exhibit when it comes to the powerful technology of social media platforms.

Many executives do engage in some social media platforms. Some are blogging, using Facebook, Twitter and LinkedIn, but studies show they are not using these forums with a real understanding for how to get the most return on their investment of time. Are they wasting precious time or, even worse, causing real damage without even knowing it?

In fact, many Fortune 100 companies who have put a toe in the water of social media are blindly spinning their wheels. The PR firm Burson-Marsteller found in a study they did of Fortune 100 companies (August 2009) that 54 percent of the Fortune 100 have a Twitter presence, compared to only 32 percent who have a blog, and 29 percent who have an active Facebook Page. Seventy-six percent of companies stick with just

one platform and of these, the top choice is Twitter. (see Chart 1 and Chart 2 below.)

CHART 1: Social Media Use in Fortune 100 Companies

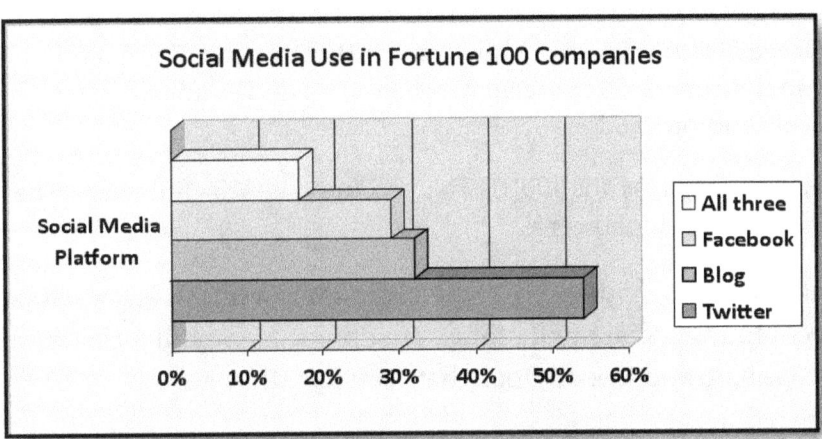

Chart 2: How Fortune 100 Companies Use Twitter

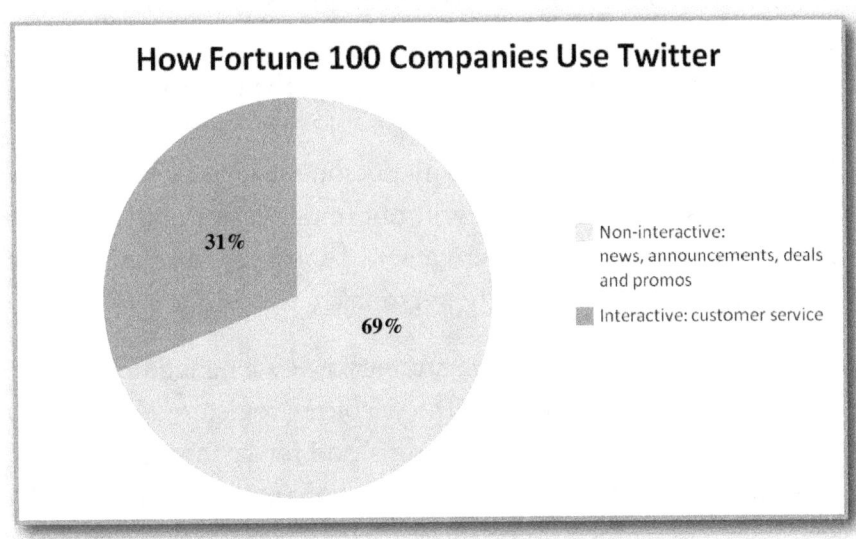

The report goes on to detail further insight into how Fortune 100 companies are using social media:

- Only 17 percent use all three mediums: Twitter, Facebook, and a blog

- Of the Fortune 100 companies on Twitter, 94 percent use it for news/announcements, 67 percent for customer service, and 57 percent for deals and promotions

- The average Fortune 100 Twitter account has 5,234 followers. The median is 674 followers

The data provides evidence that the companies who are brave enough to delve into the social media forest are doing so without a guide, often without a plan, and it is obvious that they just don't get it.

A study released in November of 2009 by Weber Shandwick, showed that most Fortune 100 Companies are using the platform in a way that is ineffective and counterproductive: "Though 73 of 100 companies had at least one registered Twitter account (up from the 54 reported in the aforementioned study released in August), the majority of them weren't using Twitter effectively to engage their followers, weren't tweeting often, and didn't display any personality in their tweets." These companies utilized Twitter without understanding that the point is to show personality. Or they activated a Twitter account without first developing an identified company personality (i.e., brand).

One major result of this ineffective strategy is low engagement from followers. "Out of the 540 total Twitter accounts registered by Fortune 100 companies, 68 percent of the accounts had fewer than 1,000 followers, 50 percent of the accounts had fewer than 500 followers and another 15 percent weren't being used at all." These statistics show the

futility of using social media platforms without first knowing how they work, and without developing a coherent plan to maximize the benefits specific to your company. In "real life" none of those companies would enter a new market without first understanding the specific demographics, psychographics, and culture of that market. Yet, that's exactly what they've done with social media.

Interestingly, small companies that develop a unified strategy generate more powerful results with social media than the big box, Fortune 500 firms have been able to do thus far. One great example is Gary Vaynerchuk's wine business. He rebranded his family's liquor business into a wine library, and through the use of social media created a multi-million dollar empire with worldwide reach. He recently wrote a book called Crush It! in which he says,

> Everything has changed. The social media revolution has irreversibly changed the way we live our lives and conduct our business. There are billions of dollars in advertising money online, waiting to be claimed by whoever can build the best content and communities." He also wisely reminds us that "Social media isn't about joining in, it's about being involved.

Bottom Line: *It's not enough to just be on these networks or to have an account. Your company must create a unified strategy with a clear purpose and intention for each of the social media platforms. Choose to leverage those platforms which align most closely with your corporate values, brand, and overall objectives. You've got to be involved to succeed.*

Generating Results Through Action Steps #1: EMBRACE CHANGE

If the old saying is true, "The only thing that stays the same is change," why do so many leaders resist change? When the results of change are misunderstood, fear kicks in and even good leaders resist the inevitable.

The great news is we have a quick remedy for such fear regarding social media: A clear understanding of best practices surrounding social media is an excellent way to turn fear into assets! The following steps outline a game plan to get you and your company started using social media effectively to maximize returns.

1. Brainstorming session. Bring together five team members who have a basic understanding of social media. Brainstorm around both the purpose for engaging and potential results expected within the next six months. You can create a task force or committee to do some due diligence about whether or not your company could benefit from being active in the social media space. Then determine both the immediate and long-term actions you'll take.

2. Open forum. Bring everyone together to discuss the action plan for social media, share the top five action steps, ask for feedback and discover who's interested in being a part of the new plan. Ask them: What is our current purpose for engaging in social media? What do we intend to use each of the platforms to accomplish?

3. Hire (or select) someone to be in charge of social media. Look around your office – who seems to really understand social media? Who knows how to leverage technology yet has a marketing and customer engagement sensibility? Who in your organization is already effectively using Linked In, Twitter, or Facebook? Select three

to five employees to present to the executive team about how social media works, how it relates to your business strategy, how it might align with your business models or brands, and how your company can leverage it.

4. Create a strategy for your company, or bring in consultative help to customize a strategy for your organization. Give the person selected two weeks to devote entirely to generating a plan to present to you. If possible, provide additional support to the person you select.

5. Lay out the plan. Determine who is responsible for each component of new plan, how the results will be measured and reward team members with the greatest success.

Also, follow the research and literature being generated on the corporate use of social media. Many helpful articles will point you in the right direction and lead you away from virtual pitfalls.

For example, Soren Gordhamer points out a crucial element many Fortune 500 companies overlook when it comes to their use of social media:

> When these companies do take a look at their strategy and use of social media, they need to realize that the key element missing is conversation. Twitter, and social media in general, is about two-way communication, which is something that all companies need to realize as they constantly evaluate and tweak their social media use.

❖

Chapter Two:
CONVERSATION

You could complain about a bad

experience online, and your message

can go viral — in seconds.

Chapter 2: CONVERSATION

In the past, marketing was done through the use of one-way, targeted messages, such as billboards, commercials, etc. Companies enjoyed the luxury of telling customers their product or service was best. But now, with the aid of social media, consumers are talking back and they demand to be heard.

With the sudden emergence of social media as an advertising tool, marketing is now a conversation between consumers and companies all vying to be the next favorite. The landscape for marketing has shifted and many are scrambling to learn new, more effective ways of utilizing interactive communication techniques and technologies.

"We are very sensitive to the zeitgeists that drive different social media outlets," says Duke Energy's Director of Marketing Communications, Scott Pacer. "We want to make sure we offer something of value – be it information, access to a product, or customer service – that enhances that outlet. We want to make sure we are developing relationships and partnerships, and not just creating another series of one-way communications."

Social media has become a new venue for marketing, but more than the opportunity to be "on message" and broadcast billboards to more arenas, social media allows for a full communication loop with various audiences simultaneously for the first time. You can now engage with your markets, have conversations, and receive instantaneous feedback in response to your marketing initiatives. Consumers now expect to share their opinion, whether you ask for it or not. Search each social media platform for mentions of your brands, products, or company name and see what's already being said!

In his book Wisdom 2.0, Soren Gordhamer notes that "with sites like Facebook and Twitter, we all essentially have our own broadcasting network, and businesses are beginning to see that rather than spending millions of dollars on traditional ad campaigns, small acts can be more valuable because people will inevitably share such experiences through the social web." Even Pepsi opted for a social media campaign instead of the coveted Superbowl ad space!

In the past, if we had a very bad or very good experience with a company, it could take days or weeks to tell all of our friends and relatives about it. Today, in a matter of minutes, we can let all our friends on Facebook or followers on Twitter know about what happened. According to Torben Rick, "When every customer experience can be easily and widely broadcast, small issues become super important." Imagine, for a moment, that you had a very bad experience with a product or company. You could complain about it online, and if you happen to be funny or engaging in the way you depict the experience, your message can go viral[3]—in seconds.

Social media has also grown exponentially because of the global financial economic challenges; social media is web 2.0 (interactive internet) at its best. Anybody, anywhere, at any time, can engage with others for free. It levels the playing field. "The best" is up for grabs and depends in large part on how well companies can nurture and maintain relationships through dialogue.

---

3 To "go viral" is a metaphor and refers to the speed and efficiency users can broadcast opinions and experiences on Twitter and Facebook, much like a virus is spread from friend to friend among humans. For the sake of example, if we assume each person has 10 followers or friends, then one post goes to my 10 friends, who each post it again so it's then seen by each of their sets of 10 friends (100 people), each of whom repeat the post and it's then seen by their 10 friends (1000 people) and so on. Within seconds, millions of people can be exposed to one bit of juicy content.

Social media allows for marketing agility and two-way communication with your customers, stakeholders, vendors, and community. Without a clear plan, your company and your products could fail miserably. On the other hand, with clear and consistent messaging, conversing, and engaging through the use of social media, your company's new product or service could become the most successful in the history of your company.

CRITICAL ERROR #2: Lack Of Community Engagement

One of the biggest mistakes companies make is to underestimate the power of social media and fail to build relationships with customers. Companies who restrict themselves to traditional one-way marketing, or keep their messages static on social media interfaces stand to lose out to competitors utilizing interactive discussion-based forums.

Presently, everyone is looking to be engaged. Customers expect to have a say in what's working or not working, and they expect to do it publicly online. They want to see what others are saying about your product/service, and they even want to talk directly with your company. Those that get a good (or bad) reception to their comments, concerns and complaints share their experience, for better or worse.

Melissa Rowley, a writer for the popular Social Media Guide site Mashable, puts it well when she writes, "There was a time when

companies issued press releases, and operated under the impression that they controlled the message of their brand. Those days are gone. Today, the brand image is linked to the thoughts and conversations of a company's consumers. Therefore, businesses must get to know their constituents."

Barry Judge, Chief Marketing Officer at Best Buy, says, You're talking with customers, you're not talking at customers. You can't control the message. You're part of the conversation, you're part of the thing that's being said about your brand and you don't get to tell customers what they get to think anymore. Consumers are giving us all kinds of information if we choose to listen to it; on Twitter, on Facebook, on our blogs; it's an incredibly valuable source for us to glean what people want!"

The art of crafting and controlling messaging about your brand or product is not relevant in the age of social media. People may already be talking about your brand, your products, your service, your company, and if you are not engaged in interactions with your community on social media, you could be missing critical data points.

CASE STUDY: *While You Were Offline*

Do you know what is being said RIGHT NOW about your company on Twitter? Does your company have a Company Page on Linked In that you don't even know about? Did someone in your firm create a

Facebook Group, and do you know what's being said in there about your organization? Do you have employees innocently blogging about highly confidential trade secrets? Did someone start a Facebook fan page for one of your products?

The most famous example of the democratic power of social media is the story of how Coca Cola got a company Facebook Fan Page. Two regular guys in Los Angeles (Dusty Sorg and Michael Jedrzejewski) who love Coke (but didn't at that time work for the company) decided to create fan page about their favorite drink. They weren't the only ones; there are over 250 fan pages for Coca Cola, none of which were created by the company. What was different about Sorg and Jedrzejewski is that their page grew to over a million fans, garnering the notice and interest of the executives at Coke.

When Facebook started enforcing a policy that only allows people authorized or associated with a company to make a branded "page," the Coke folks hired Dusty and Mike. The Coca Cola fan page is now the 2nd most popular fan page (Barack Obama is first), with over 4.1 million fans.

If, as in the case of Coca Cola, you find that someone who is not authorized by your company has created a Facebook fan page for your brand or product, you do have options and can either ask Facebook or the owners of the page to transfer ownership to you or simply ask Facebook to shut down the page. Of course, if the owner of the page is doing a great job at building and engaging the community, you may wish to go the route of Coca Cola and partner with the fan who created the page.

Bottom Line: By sparking authentic and transparent conversations via social media, companies can get to know their consumers, learn what their stakeholders expect of them and capitalize on customers' enthusiasm.

Generating Results Through Action Steps #2: ENGAGE

If you want people to go out and talk about your company, engage them in conversation. To do this you must be visible and have a lively interactive presence on at least one of the social media platforms.

Weber Shandwick prescribes five essential steps as a starting point for Fortune 100 companies to create true engagement and market interaction on Twitter, although we assert that these very steps are exactly the points we'd prescribe for leveraging social media on any platform in any company:

1. Listen to conversations

2. Participate in conversations

3. Update frequently with valuable information

4. Reply to people who talk about issues that are important to your company

5. Retweet – or pass along with attribution – relevant conversations

Not only is the conversation two-way, so is the relationship. What companies learn from their customers through social media conversations is invaluable and could potentially revolutionize the way they do business. Jennifer Leggio of ZDNet surveyed top executives on the value of interaction with customers through social media. Carlos Dominguez, a senior vice president at Cisco, attests to this phenomenon, "We see social media, such as blogs, as a great way to build your business and tap into the ideas and input of people using your products."

Charles Miller, Director of Social Media Strategy at DirectTV affirms the mutual benefit of virtual conversation. "What we learn from customers online allows us to be resilient and in sync with what they want . . . It's a dynamic push-pull that is much faster and more direct than other forms of feedback."

"The more we engage with our consumers, the more we learn and the more we can expand our social media efforts," says Bert Dumars, Vice President of E-business and Interactive Marketing for Newell Rubbermaid. "I cannot emphasize enough how important it is to start small, be flexible and be willing to pull back and change if something does not work."

It is crucial to keep in mind that people seek honesty and true feeling in their relationships; they seek this with their favorite brands as well. You cannot program a robot to respond to Facebook or Twitter feeds. Nor can companies expect to dominate the conversation and tell consumers what to think. Absolute transparency, no holds barred, is key.

Entrepreneur Jeffrey Hollender, the Executive Chairperson of the green products company Seventh Generation, says most corporations are not nearly transparent enough. "It's a mistake for companies to

think that they cannot tell the truth and hide anything they do," said Hollender. "Whether it's a customer, or an employee, or a reporter, someone will disclose a corporation's dirty little secrets."

Related to transparency, it is essential to avoid using a "straw man" or fake persona as your social media front. Consumers won't be fooled and you will lose face by not revealing your true face. Here are some concrete steps to get the conversation started:

1.   Select a great conversationalist, who understands social media, to be in charge of "listening" to what your customers are saying about your brand. Give this person the leeway to offer freebees and apologies for bad experiences. Empower your Social Media Lead to engage in conversations as him or herself, but on behalf of the organization, so that there is a personal connection with a real human being.

2.   Get your company leaders involved. Customers want to know they have direct access to having a dialogue with the top leadership inside every company. This ensures they can share ideas and gripe, if necessary. They also want to feel like they are "in the know" and have access to the latest insider information.

3.   Get involved in the real world through the virtual community. Select a local charity that fits your organization's values or your team's interests and begin supporting them – both financially and on social media. Bring awareness to their cause and what you're doing to support them. Or, select a company or leader with whom you have a strategic alliance to promote on social media. If you set about increasing a partner's exposure on social media, you'll gain more influence than if you are simply "on message" tooting your own company's horn.

4. Engage your community by asking for input, demonstrating that you respond to their comments and questions online, being visible, inviting participation in members, and anything else you can think to do to make your brand or organization real, personable, approachable, and responsive. Engage consistently with your community or don't bother using social media. ❖

Chapter Three:
EMPLOYEE MANAGEMENT

Chapter 3: CONVERSATION

Social Media is so popular and pervasive that, chances are, your employees are already using it for their own purposes. Many companies are reluctant to incorporate social media for fear of lost productivity and employees "wasting time" by checking their own pages and status. Anxiety about breaches in security through social media also strengthens this fear.

Some companies even ban the personal use of social media while on the job. However, the time and energy it takes to enforce such protocol could be better spent developing programs to leverage employee passion for social media towards the company's best interests and brand promotion on such platforms.

Some companies embrace the use of social media and manage it to their advantage by establishing their own internal equivalents. According to Chief Learning Officer Magazine at IBM, the company boasts "17,000 internal blogs, 53,000 employees on its internal version of Facebook, and 500,000 participants in crowdsourcing jams[1] who have helped develop 10 incubator businesses with the potential of reaching $100 million."

---

1 "Crowdsourcing" refers to online suggestion boxes, which can generate an enormous volume of ideas and feedback. Crowdsourcing jams are forums of such ideas that operate at will, or internally within a business. It is the virtual way to brainstorm.

CRITICAL ERROR #3: Banning
The Use Of Social Media

According to a study commissioned by Robert Half Technology, "54 percent of U.S. companies say they've banned workers from using social networking sites like Twitter, Facebook, LinkedIn and MySpace, while on the job."

Many of these companies do not use social media at the corporate level to engage consumers and the employee community. According to a 2009 report by Russell Herder, company reputation, security and confidentiality deter the implementation of social media platforms. A shocking 51% of companies surveyed who have banned social media say the reason is "simply not knowing enough about it."

Meanwhile, according to the Robert Half study, "A survey of 237 corporate employees showed that 77 percent of workers who have a Facebook account use it during work hours." This 77 percent is perhaps the most important statistic, revealing the pervasive quality of social media despite corporate bans. Even if employees are technically blocked from using the platforms at work, they log in hours of their own time, generating content that could be useful, or harmful, to their employers.

Bottom Line: Banning social media may be tempting, given security or productivity concerns, but it doesn't actually work, since your employees are likely to continue their use of social networks on BlackBerries, iPhones, Androids and the like. If you want to completely ban it, you may have to confiscate cell phones at the office door!

Again, the best approach is acceptance and strategy, which leads to leveraging the power of the social media monster to benefit your company.

 Generating Results Through Action Steps #3: Engage Employee Passion in Social Media Policy

It's important to recognize your employees are likely to use social media on their own, whether or not it is "safe" to use within your organization. Thus, creating a baseline is essential. Determine what's acceptable to share on social media without compromising security positions or trade secrets.

1. Pull together examples of what's good and not good to share on social media – and explain why. Rather than simply being told what they can or cannot share on social media, your employees deserve to know why any company would tell them what to do with their own time. You'll get their buy-in by honesty and real-world examples.

2. Once the ground rules are set, get employee feedback on how they can use their social media experience at work and on their own time to further the mission and vision of your organization.

3. Consumers desire authenticity, so it's important to allow employees to be authentic as well.

4. Keep in mind that employees are "internal customers" and as such, they too will have a voice outside of work on social media about their opinions and concerns as employees.

"Forget the unified company image, give staff the freedom to be themselves, and trust that the relationships that they build will help the company in the long run," says Soren Gordhamer, author of Wisdom 2.0. In this way, your employees "put a friendly face on the corporation" and become one of your companies best marketing resources. Not to mention, imagine the difference it will make for your company's retention when employees begin sharing how well they are treated.

❖

Chapter Four:
POLICY AND OVERSIGHT

Soldiers utilize Facebook to

communicate with one another

with unprecedented success.

Chapter 4: POLICY AND OVERSIGHT

When your employees understand the value of social media, their time spent on Facebook, Twitter, MySpace or Linked In could prove to be a gold mine.

But, as discussed in the previous chapter, it's important to establish ground rules before going live, or social media could do more harm than good. Clear communication regarding the use of social media could save your company thousands of dollars in marketing. A lack of understanding resulting from unclear communication could result in branding and security hazards for your company.

Ground rules for social media practices will depend on your industry. An extreme example of this struggle to establish policies that protect while still utilizing the advantages of social media is occurring right now in the military. According to the Combined Arms Center Blog, the military is struggling with the question of whether or not to ban social media altogether because of security concerns. Many military insiders feel a total ban would ultimately put the armed forces at a disadvantage.

The Army currently has a Facebook page with 43,000 fans. Soldiers and their commanders utilize the platform to communicate with one another with unprecedented two-way success. COL Meyerowich, author of the post, "Overcoming Our Fears of Social Media," points out that young soldiers also use social media on a daily basis, and just as a young officer is trained to protect a physical boundary, he or she can be enabled to protect a virtual one as well. The military has "a history of solving complex problems," Meyerowich says, and social media is a monster the military can tame with proper protocol. He

challenges leaders to creatively work towards "solutions that minimize risks without hampering the ability to utilize all the good that Web 2.0 applications can provide."

CRITICAL ERROR #4:
Lack Of Clear Social Media Policy

Without clear guidance, your employees will not know how best to utilize social media tools for business reasons. Just as you ensure the right person with the right message is serving as the spokesperson for your company, you want to ensure everyone is clear about how to use social media to bolster profits, solidify desired branding and generate trust with your customers.

You also want to know what your folks are saying out there in social media land, because they may be talking about how much they hate (or love) their boss, their company, their job, etc. They may be revealing trade secrets or tipping off competitors by sharing business intelligence without realizing it. They may be inadvertently speaking out against the very controls and messaging you crafted to align with the corporate mission, vision and values.

For example, a disgruntled employee of a large non-profit was complaining about her boss on her Facebook account. Apparently she had forgotten that she had previously, in better times, "friended" her

boss, who could now see all of her complaints. Her comments were so inflammatory, that her boss not only wanted to fire her, but wanted to sue her for defamation, and the HR director of the organization had a new challenge on her hands.

Whether or not you can fire an employee for comments made on Facebook is another lurking monster challenging businesses in the private and public sectors. The issue has implications that reverberate through human resource practices, employment law and internal policy.

Regardless, social media is not only a powerful tool for gaining insight about the morale of your employees, it can also be helpful to your organization in recruiting and hiring processes as well. Just think how much more you can learn about a prospective employee from the posts on their Facebook page. Wouldn't you love to know if they have a track record of speaking ill of their boss and co-workers before you hire them?

Facebook can also be a valuable resource for understanding your team members. Perhaps you've suspected for months that Jane in accounting is having some kind of a personal crisis. Before Facebook, you'd never have known if she was coping with a divorce, sick child, ailing parent, or other personal challenge. You may have felt uncomfortable asking, not wanting to pry into personal affairs. If Jane has discussed her crisis on Facebook, you can offer support and resources to assist her, or at the very least be understanding and compassionate as to her diminished focus at work.

Bottom Line: Without a social media policy, and implementation of tools and systems to monitor and enforce that policy, your company is open to real risks in real time in the real world. To best leverage social media, it must relate to

and be part of your business strategy in order to ensure that everyone who is on the same team stays on the same page.

Generating Results Through Action Steps #4: CREATE A POSITIVE POLICY

Create a social media policy for your employees that allows them to leverage the platforms for the advancement of the company, rather than for their own social uses. If you need help developing a social media policy, the online database, Social Media Governance, has links to more than 100 policies across industries. You can filter by industry, and search the documents.

Sharlyn Lauby (president of Internal Talent Management (ITM)) posted 10 'must-haves' for your social media policy. These 10 tips will help you steer clear of pitfalls and allow you and your team to focus on what's important: engaging the customer.

1. Introduce the purpose of social media

2. Be responsible for what you write

3. Be authentic

4. Consider your audience

5. Exercise good judgment

6. Understand the concept of community

7. Respect copyrights and fair use

8. Remember to protect confidential & proprietary info

9. Bring value

10. Productivity matters

"One of the common themes I kept coming across in introductions to social media policies," Lauby observes, "is the idea that the policy should focus on the things that employees can do rather than what they can't do."

Here are some more concrete steps to get you started creating and introducing your policy:

- Accentuate the positive and use praise to guide employees. For those who are voluntarily saying great things about your company on social media, praise them, recognize them, showcase them. Some employees will take the initiative (without your request) to talk about how great his/her boss/employer is – reward and celebrate this behavior.

- When crafting your policy, keep it simple and to the point, using real-world examples, and focusing on what employees can and should do rather than the negative. Consider the tips above. It's essential that your employees first understand why the social media policy is important. Otherwise, it's unlikely you'll gain their immediate acceptance. On the contrary, if they feel like they are a part of creating the policy, you're more likely to gain immediate buy-in. In working with your team, be sure your social media policy is aligned and congruent with your overall business strategy, and supports your objectives for your company.

- Create a policy that is flexible. Social media is brand new to many organizations, and it evolves every second. Even after you create your social media policy, it's likely events will occur that will provide excellent material for updating your policy. Every event that causes disruption is the perfect opportunity to learn what does and does not work. For whatever reason, people need to know why. Be sure to give the "why" when the policy is first enacted and as you update the policy along the way. Reason is the only way to build consensus. Control may only cause irritation, while clear data and consensus creates buy-in. When it comes time to train employees on your new policy, you will meet with cooperation rather than irritation.

Chapter Five:
TRAINING

Chapter 5: TRAINING

Even with the best policy in the world, lack of employee training on social media could be disastrous for your company. Social media leaves the door wide open; everything makes an impression, and impressions are broadcast over wide audiences, for better or worse.

Effective training and monitoring are crucial. It takes effort and dedication to balance the corporate mission and brand with the authentic relationships forged on social media.

 *CRITICAL ERROR #5: Lack Of Training And Resources Dedicated To Branding And Relationship Management Through Social Media*

Does your company have staff dedicated to monitoring conversations happening within social media platforms, and are they fully equipped to protect your company's branding? How about the branding of your executives? Or the branding of your individual products or services?

Do your employees know how to use all the features social media has to offer? And do they recognize the unforgiving consequences of an errant post? Often times, people simply post notes without really understanding who will see them or how it will affect them or their company.

Social media allows every employee and every customer the potential equivalent of setting up a virtual billboard about your company. You can't control when or where that billboard will go up, you can't even control what it will say.

On social media platforms, every post is public and it matters. Training employees on policy and monitoring your company's presence online could prevent the negative consequences a stray tweet could hold for your company.

Kris Colvin of Design for Users makes a business case for implementing employee social media training, sharing an example of a Starbucks employee who used Flickr to post a gallery of pictures entitled "87th and Sunset: Life at Starbucks." These albums included pictures of his customers taken on the sly, some captioned with negative and demeaning comments. From this circumstance, Colvin draws the following lessons, which help organizations figure out where to draw the line when monitoring and training employees:

It's unreasonable to expect:

1. Employees not to tweet, post to Facebook, Flickr, YouTube or any other social site.

2. Employees not to occasionally have a work gripe that gets aired.

3. Employees to turn over the keys to all their social sites so you can monitor them like Big Brother.

4. Employees not to want to share/bond with colleagues via pics, funny videos, etc. (not all the pics in the Flickr set used as this bad example are inappropriate or problematic).

It is reasonable to expect:

1. Employees will not deliberately bash your brand on public forums and if they do they run the risk of losing their jobs.

2. Employees will make sure their personal artifacts online don't tarnish your brand and they will clean up what does if their name is associated with your company.

3. Employees will realize they are representatives of your company whether they're on the clock or not, and behave with some decorum.

4. Employees won't bash, disrespect or call customers names.

5. Employees won't threaten customers.

6. Employees won't do things to deliberately humiliate customers, such as take their picture or video them without permission.

Bottom Line: Colvin cautions:

> If you do NOT have a training program in place, get it in place now! You don't have time to waste, and it doesn't have to be hard. You can make improvements as you go along. Start with your managers and hold them accountable for ensuring employees do the right thing when it comes to both playing online AND collecting a paycheck from your company.

 *Generating Results*
Through Action Steps #5: TRAINING

Training on social media offers a safe outlet for your employees to share what they want to share and keep your brand shining!

Train your people how to use social media in ways that are both authentic expressions and official representations of your company. Empower your team to leverage the tools at their fingertips on behalf of your goals and objectives.

Designate. Who is best suited to provide training on social media? The "best" person could be a consulting company who specializes in social media training. Likewise, the best person could be someone within your organization who understands social media, is willing to gain additional training, create training for others within your organization and serve as the go-to person for questions.

Update. Social media, along with all technology, is constantly changing. That said, it's important to ensure your social media go-to people are consistently taking courses to upgrade their skills and share them with the rest of your organization.

Empower. Not only is it important that your employees understand how to use social media, it's equally important they are clear about what to share that could make a difference for your organization. When they have great experiences, ensure they know to share about them on social media.

RECAP:
Action Steps
To Tame The Media

RECAP: Action Steps To Tame The Social Media Monster

Action Step One: Embrace Change

Social media also provides up-to-date information on your industry. Are you capitalizing on the opportunity to learn and stay ahead of the curve? Are you missing out on valuable, and potentially free, media exposure? Explore how social media might benefit your organization in handling a crisis, contribute to marketing, or expediting broad-reach communication needs. Leverage relationships on social media to find new vendors, suppliers, and talent. Create advocates, agents, and raving fans for your company, product, or service. Gather business intelligence on competitors and set the stage for strategic alliances.

Action Step Two: Join The Conversation Change

Learn what customers expect and what they are already saying about your company. Engage them in dialogue and respond to their feedback.

Action Step Three: Be Authentic

Allow your employees to be themselves as the "friendly face of your company." Be transparent and build the company brand.

Action Step Four: Create a Policy and a Plan for Social Media

Don't ban the social media monster. Learn to channel its power.

Action Step Five: Educate Your Employees on the Consequences and Power of the Social Media

Teach them that their contributions matter to the bottom line.

Bottom Line: Just Do It! Get on social media, get involved and engage with others.

"I was a Twitter skeptic until I started doing it about 10 months ago. Now I have more than 26,000 followers, many of whom tweet me to say what products they like and don't like. I spend a lot of time each day responding to those messages, because they're the folks I learn from the most. They are virtual focus groups," says Kathy Ireland in the December 2009/January 2010 issue of Inc Magazine.

Want to find out what your customers think about your product, company and your employees?

Engage them in a conversation!

❖

CONCLUSION

CONCLUSION

The number of active Twitter users in the United States alone already exceeds 25 million and can be expected to continue to grow, while the worldwide figure jumps to more than 45 million users. On LinkedIn there are 60 million users. On Facebook, there are more than 350 million users. This is a massive human database to tap; companies that understand the value of social media can benefit from its potential as a viable engagement strategy on multiple levels.

Social Media is a monster growing quickly and changing the landscape forever. It is a monster that must be faced in today's marketplace, or the consequences are brutal.

"Companies can no longer hide behind their brand," says Lisa Agona, Chief Marketing Officer for Lexis Nexis Risk Solutions, whose team has rebranded the $1.5 billion company over the last year. "Clients used to have to ask for recommendations from companies that provided testimonials from people they knew would say nice things." But thanks to web 2.0 technologies like blogs, social networks, and Google, consumers can get unfiltered reviews straight from the horse's mouth. "So delivering on your brand's promise is even more critical. If you don't, someone will say so."

Despite this revolutionary climate, the Weber Shandwick study cited above concludes that for the majority of Fortune 100 companies, Twitter still remains a missed opportunity. Many of their Twitter accounts did not appear to listen to or engage with their readers, instead offering a one-way broadcast of press releases, company blog posts and event information. This falls short of the opportunity that Twitter

offers as a valuable communications channel and strategic social network.

However, with a little creativity, the right resources, planning, training and incentives, social media is a monster easily tamed as long as companies:

- Create a companywide engagement strategy; a set of guidelines with best practices

- Demonstrate a consistent and comprehensive brand presence

- Build a dialogue that paves the way to new relationships with customers and advocates

- Generate loyalty among new and existing communities

Don't be swallowed whole by the beast of social media. Put it to work for you!

Whether you use social media to gather business intelligence, to stalk a competitor, to listen to your market, to find new resources or deals, to recruit employees, or to engage your customers, it can expand your business, enhance your employee morale, retention and productivity, and help your company to leverage the Internet in majestic fashion.

Social media need not be a monster that keeps you up at night! Someone in your organization has already tamed it and can put those skills to work for your company. The important thing to keep in mind is that you don't have to have it all thought through to perfection before you engage. Due to the nature of social media and how quickly the face of

web 2.0 is changing, you can learn on the go, in real time, as you seek to integrate the rewards and benefits of social media into your company's activities.

MEET THE AUTHORS

Suzi Pomerantz, MT, MCC, Innovative Leadership International, LLC.

Suzi Pomerantz, CEO of Innovative Leadership International LLC, is an award-winning executive coach, facilitator, and author with over 18 years experience coaching and teaching leaders and teams in over 150 organizations internationally across Government Agencies and private sector clients, including seven companies on the Fortune 100 list and 7 corporate law departments.

Suzi specializes in the intersection between leadership and business development and helps executives, teams and high-potential future leaders to clarify their vision and exceed prior performance. She was one of the first executive coaches to receive the Master credential from the International Coach Federation over 14 years ago and is considered a thought leader in the coaching industry. She serves on multiple international Boards of Directors and Advisory Boards in the coaching industry, and has authored 25 publications about coaching, ethics, and business development, including her book Seal the Deal. She received the 2007 Woman of Achievement Award from Business and Professional Women with the Commission for Women. In 2008 the ICCO Board of Directors established a legacy award: the Suzi Pomerantz Award for Stewardship is given annually. In 2009, Suzi was named the #1 Most Influential Executive Coach on Twitter. In 2010 Suzi was invited to be a founding coach for the Relationship Masters Academy.

www.suzipomerantz.com

❖

Misti Burmeister, Inspirion, LLC.

Misti Burmeister, CEO and Founder of Inspirion, LLC, is an award-winning entrepreneur and best-selling author of "From Boomer to Bloggers: Success Strategies Across Generations" and the accompanying workbook "From Boomer to Bloggers: Workbook and Resources." She is a recognized expert in communication with a niche in generational diversity. As an expert in intergenerational communication, Burmeister has worked with Fortune 500 companies and top military leaders to motivate and inspire their staff to work together, beyond generational differences. Burmeister believes increased understanding creates increased collaboration and she supports this process through motivational speaking, executive coaching and customized training programs.

www.InspirionInc.com

❖

OTHER LEARNING
MATERIALS
FROM THE AUTHORS

CHECK OUT OTHER LEARNING MATERIALS FROM THE AUTHORS

SEAL THE DEAL NETWORKING:
How Coaches Connect With Leaders In The Age Of Social Media

By Suzi Pomerantz, MT., MCC. $9.97

We live in the Age of Social Meedia. This book will tell you all you need to know about the critical mindsets for how to leverage social media to your networking advantage! Learn from The #1 Most Influential Executive Coach on Twitter (according to WeFollow.com) how coaches and leaders connect.

Here's a sneak peek at what's in the 50-page e-book:

Table of Contents

Introduction

The global economy has changed everything. The game is different in the Age of Social Media because now it's not enough to have great business cards and go to networking meetings, smile and shake a few hands, meet and greet a few movers and shakers, practice the old elevator pitch. We have to be visible and engaged on Linked In, Facebook and Twitter. We have to engage people on a blog. We have to manage our online reputation. We have to network internationally and in multiple platforms simultaneously. We have to network ALL THE TIME! Networking is not what we thought it was just a few short years ago. Coaching is one of those businesses where regardless of whether you sell B2B or B2C, your networking skills are now as critical if not more so than your coaching skills. Leadership requires mastery of networking and social media with

a strategic understanding of how they intersect so that you can effectively lead your team, employees, volunteers, or coaching clients.

NOW WHAT?!

Relax, I'm here to help. This eBook was created in response to the changing face of networking, especially to help you learn to navigate the new landscape easily so that you can focus on what you do best, which is coach your clients and lead your business!

This eBook will cover the basic mindsets of real life networking, and show you how to leverage and integrate those mindsets and practices into social networking online. The good news is that you are not alone. The better news is that you don't have to figure it out all by yourself or reinvent any wheels. This handy little guide will show you the fun and easy way to get your networking game on and play with the free tools available in order to grow your leads, prospects, clients, and ultimately your profits.

THE CATCH...

Of course, you will have to bypass your fears, concerns, and doubts about your capacity to network like a pro and expand your confidence and competencies in the direction of your ideal vision for your coaching practice/coaching business. You will have to get in the game because this is a sport with no bench. You will probably have to let go of a few limiting beliefs about how it should be. And in order to succeed you will have to lighten up and have fun. Yes, you must enjoy yourself. So there.

YOU CAN DO IT!

Lots of folks are coaches these days, have you noticed? While it may be easy to become a coach, getting your calendar filled with coaching clients is a skillset often overlooked by most of the coach training programs out there. Of course, you can always use the book Seal the Deal as your business development training, but Networking is the critical first step and the go-to action for starting, growing, and unsticking your coaching business. When I wrote Seal the Deal, social media hadn't yet exploded onto the scene and there is nothing in that book about this incredibly important business development opportunity! That's why I'm releasing this eBook. We've excerpted some of the best core concepts on networking from Seal the Deal, updated it, revised it, improved it, re-worked it, and added to the topic so that you can quickly get rocking in social media with ease and joy.

Networking is no longer something you do when you are thinking about growing your business. Networking in the age of social media means that you have the opportunity to be plugged in 24/7 and if you are not taking advantage of that opportunity you are leaving money on the table.

Purchase your copy here for only $9.97

http://www.suzipomerantz.com/products-page/

FROM BOOMERS TO BLOGGERS:

Success Strategies Across Generations

by Misti Burmeister, MA $17.95

Writer's Digest: "From Boomer to Bloggers is a comprehensive treatise that every experienced manager and new employee should read.

Burmeister culls years of experience and expertise in a short, easy-to-read book that is sure to help bridge the annoying generation gap that is likely to continue expanding in officess and workplaces across the world."

Here's a sneak peek at what's in the book:

Table Of Contents

Introduction

Are you a young professional looking for assistance in navigating your organization's environment, communicating with seasoned professionals, and moving your career forward?

As a seasoned professional, have you ever wondered how to best tap into and utilize the talents and skills of the youngest generation? Have you wondered how to get them to care about their work, show up on time and do what needs to get done without complaining about flextime, holidays or promotions?

What if you learned everything you needed to know to effectively motivate, inspire and create results within every generation?

What if every employee wanted to be led by you? What if every company and leader wanted you on their team? What if you were more employable, rather than merely employed?

Have you wondered how companies like Google and Disney have created an environment to retain their talent? How about award-winning companies like Post Properties? Post is a national property management company that has created an award-winning internship program which sources a talent pool of dedicated employees for their future. This book will give you insight into how these winning corporations have kept their most valuable resources – their people, and how their people find fulfillment in their work.

Purchase your copy here for only $17.95

http://synergypressonline.com/booksore.php

About
Innovative
Leadership International

Innovative Leadership International LLC (ILI) is a woman-owned executive coaching firm specializing in organizational coaching, leadership development, and business development. The master coaches and consultants of ILI provide executive coaching, team coaching, and emerging leader coaching in organizations to assist executives and their teams with setting strategic direction for their organizations, managing talent, and developing leadership bench strength. We help organizations develop and retain leadership capacity by coaching leaders in executive presence, presentation skills, personal power, communication, and vision work. We specialize in business development coaching for attorneys, coaches, trainers, consultants, and other professional service providers in the areas of sales, marketing, and networking. Since 1993,we have coached and trained thousands of leaders and teams in over 110 organizations internationally, including 7 Fortune 100 companies,11 law firms, and 6 corporate law departments. We help leaders clarify their vision and exceed prior performance. We help attorneys and coaches demystify the sales process and implement a systematic process for business development.We help organizations improve communication and leadership, transforming cultures one individual at a time. We provide coaching, training, facilitation, and leadership development services. http://www.innovativeleader.com Innovative Leadership International LLC (ILI) is a woman-owned executive coaching firm specializing in organizational coaching, leadership development and business development. ILI helps leaders and organizations find clarity in chaos. We are part of a network of strategic alliances collaborating to serve our clients' real-time leadership development needs. We develop leaders by delivering outstanding value and service consistent with our commitment to organizational excellence, professionalism, integrity, and performance. We work in partnership

with our clients to transform organizations through in-dividuals, and we have a powerful impact on the results our clients achieve. The master coaches and consultants of ILI provide executive coaching, team coaching, and emerging leader coaching in organizations to assist executives and their teams with setting strategic direction for their organizations, manag-ing talent, and developing leadership bench strength. We help organizations develop and retain leadership capacity by coaching leaders in executive presence, presentation skills, personal power, communication, and vision work. We help executives, teams and future leaders to clarify their vision, navigate the political landscape, increase their leadership capacity, hone their leader-ship brand and exceed prior performance. We help organizations to im-prove communication, impact and leadership, transforming cultures one individual at a time. We also provide business development coaching for attorneys, coaches, trainers, consultants, and other professional service providers in the areas of sales, marketing, and networking. We help attorneys and coaches to demystify the sales process and imple-ment a systematic process for business development. Our work is in service of stewardship and excellence, committed to helping our leader clients and the coaches who serve them to have a profound impact on their businesses, people, legacy, social consciousness, and the planet.

http://www.innovativeleader.com

SOURCES
AND RECOMMENDED
READING LIST

SOURCES AND RECOMMENDED READING LIST

BestBuy. (May 03, 2009) The Marketing Capability: The Future is Digital. Video posted to http://www.youtube.com/watch?v=-rTzIAWI4Ms&feature=player_embedded#

Business Blogging Blog. (April 8, 2009) Coca-Cola's Fan Page: The second most popular page on Facebook. Retrieved from http://www.socialmedia.org/blog/coca-colas-fan-page-the-second-most-popular-page-on-facebook/

Colvin, Kris. (Oct 4, 2009) A Case for Employee Social Media Training. Retrieved from http://design-for-users.com/customer-experience/employee-social-media-training/

Gordhamer, S. (September 22, 2009). 4 Ways Social Media is Changing Business. Retrieved from http://mashable.com/2009/09/22/social-media-business/

Gordhamer, S. (2009) Wisdom 2.0. HarperOne. New York, NY http://wisdom2.net

Lauby, Sharlyn. (June 2, 2009) 10 Must-Haves for Your Social Media Policy. Retrieved from http://mashable.com/2009/06/02/social-media-policy-musts/

Lavrusik, V. (Nov 17, 2009) STUDY: Most Fortune 100 Companies Don't Get Twitter. Retrieved from http:mashable.com/2009/11/17/fortune-100-companies-twitter/

Leggio, Jennifer. (May 4, 2009) Fortune 500 Series: Duke Energy drives green initiatives with social media. Retrieved from http://blogs.zdnet.com/feeds/?p=1054

Ostrow, A. (Aug 3, 2009) Twitter is Top Social Media Platform at Fortune 100 Companies. Retrieved from http://mashable.com/2009/08/03/twitter-fortune-100/

Rowley, Melissa Jun. (Nov 6, 2009) Why Social Media is Vital to Coporate Responsibility. Retrieved from http://mashable.com/2009/11/06/social-responsibility

Russel Herder and Ethos Business Law. (August 2009) Social Media:Embracing the Opportunities, Averting the Risks. Retrieved from http://www.russelherder.com/SocialMediaResearch/TCHRA_Resources/RHP_089_WhitePaper.pdf

Social Media Governance Online Database of Social Media Policies. Retrieved from http://socialmediagovernance.com/policies.php

Smith, Justin. (March 18, 2009) How Do You Treat a Fan Who Owns Your Facebook Page? Retrieved from http://www.insidefacebook.com/2009/03/18/how-do-you-treat-a-fan-who-owns-your-facebook-page/

Sweitzer, Tamara. (Nov 25, 2009) Study: Inc. 500 CEOs Aggressively Use Social Media for Business. Retrieved from http://www.inc.com/news/articles/2009/11/inc500-social-media-usage.html

Torbin, Rick. (Oct 25, 2009) Is there a change in how customers' concerns are addressed? Retrieved from http://torbenrick.eu/blog/change-management/is-there-a-change-in-how-customers%E2%80%99-concerns-are-addressed/

Vaynerchuch, Gary. (May 13, 2009) Crush it! Why Now it's the Time to Cash in on Your Passion. Video posted to http:/garyvaynerchuk.com/post/107300929/crush-it-why-now-is-the-time-to-cash-in-on-your/

Weber Shandwick Digital Communications. (November 2009) Twittervention Study of Fortune100 Companies on Twitter. Retrieved from www.webershandwick.com/resources/ws/flash/Twittervention_study.pdf

Wired Epicenter. (Oct 9, 2009) Study: 54 Percent of companies Ban Facebook, Twitter at Work. Retrieved from http://www.wired.com/epicenter/2009/10/study-54-of-companies-ban-facebook-twitter-at-work/#ixzz0d7bxMHWC

NOTES

NOTES

www.ingramcontent.com/pod-product-compliance
Lightning Source LLC
Chambersburg PA
CBHW071229170526
45165CB00003B/1045